W9-CYD-988

100 Hints:
How to Stay Married for Life

Insights From Those Married 50 Years or More!

by Bill Morelan

100 Hints: How to Stay Married for Life
Insights From Those Married 50 Years or More!
ISBN 1-57757-003-0

2nd Printing

Copyright © 1996 by The Concerned Group, Inc.
P.O. Box 1000
Siloam Springs, Arkansas 72761

Published by Trade Life Books, Inc.
P. O. Box 55325
Tulsa, Oklahoma 74155

Printed in the United States of America. All rights reserved under International Copyright Law. Contents and/or cover may not be reproduced in whole or in part in any form without the express written consent of the Publisher.

Dedication

Lovingly dedicated to Russell Potter, Sr. and his wife, Virginia — married seventy-three years and still going strong!

Special Thanks

The following people generously contributed their time, energy, and talents to the development of this edition. Sincere appreciation is extended to the following people: Judy Adkins, Cindy Blount, Sheila Blount, Meredith Church, Felicia Graham, Julie Hill, Jeanne Jensen, Sara Jensen, Rich LaVere, Russ L. Potter II, Gordon Rich, Riki Stamps, Lou Stewart, Paula Taylor, and my loving wife, Sheri. Most of all, thanks to all the wonderful people who shared their wisdom in the following pages!

Introduction

I will always remember that cold winter morning. The steely-glass doors hissed in quiet protest as I slipped softly into the nursing home. I was only in town for a few hours and felt duty-bound to visit my grandfather. Not that he'd ever know I'd been there — he'd suffered a severe stroke a few years back, and now his world was peopled only with strangers.

It was still early, and the nurse at the desk merely nodded as I explained where I was headed. My sneakers squeaked faintly as I walked down the polished hall. "I'll just see if he's awake," I thought as I peeked through the slightly-open door.

Early morning light painted highlights on the handmade quilt that covered him; his rumpled grey hair nestled in a downy pillow. And by his side sat Grandmother, steadily crocheting yet another heirloom-to-be. I'd forgotten she came here almost every morning to spend a few hours by his side.

As I paused a moment, reluctant to disturb this peaceful scene, Grandpa stirred in his sleep. In an instant, Grandma reached out and gently covered his wrinkled, work-scarred hand with her own. Two hands, clasped in an embrace born of years of struggling together towards a common goal. It's a moment I'll always remember.

I spent much longer than I'd planned in Grandpa's room that morning. Grandma and I talked about their life together — a rough life in many ways, yet the good always outweighed the bad. As we talked, I began to catch just a glimpse of the depth of true love—something few of us ever experience in today's busy, bustling world. And as I began the interviews that led to this book, those clasped, wrinkled hands were always before me.

⌒

This book celebrates the immense storehouse of wisdom and love that resides in the hearts and minds of older American couples. It's a tribute to their rugged common sense; a reflection of their good-natured banter; and a testimony to the strength of their commitment to one another.

May your heart be softened, your understanding deepened, and your relationships strengthened as you share in their lives through the following pages.

Bill Morehead

Please Note:

Quotations in this book were gathered primarily from people married fifty years or more. As far as possible, all information has been verified as factual by the author or his agents.

Hint #1

❦

"Never let a day go by without telling each other, 'I love you.'"

❦

Jack & Bernice Wein
Married: February 23, 1946
Trenton, Michigan

Jack and Bernice's sense of humor is legendary. "Bernice said if I bought one more car, I'd have to sleep in it," Jack says grinning. "I told her a man *should* have more than one bedroom!" "Instead of arguing, let the man think he's the boss," Bernice says with a wink. "Eventually he'll come around to your way of thinking."

Hint #2

"Take the days one at a time.
Soon fifty years will pass —
but it won't seem like it."

❧

Al & Evylyn Little
Married: March 3, 1946
Bellflower, Missouri

Al and Evylyn Little are committed Christians. Al works as a chaplain for the Los Angeles County jails; Evylyn loves spending time with little children.

Hint #3

*"You only get out of a marriage
what you put into it."*

Eldon & Ginny Phillips
Married: October 30, 1946
Belle Center, Ohio

Eldon and Ginny went to high school together. His first move: he stole her shoes during a play rehearsal! "It took him eight years to convince me to marry him," laughs Ginny.

Hint #4

"Love each other and share common goals."

∽

Ray & Florence Borquez
Married: November 23, 1946
Los Angeles, California

Ray and Florence remain active in church activities. Although he's technically retired, Ray still enjoys the occasional odd job. Florence considers herself lucky to have a spouse who shares her active outlook on life.

Hint #5

"Always treat your wife like a lady."

Sol & Edna Weiss
Married: June 16, 1946
New York City, New York

Sol and Edna met at a party when he was fourteen and she was thirteen. "We still hold hands," Sol says. "And I still put up with his sense of humor," Edna laughs.

Hint #6

༥

*"Have a sense of humor and learn
to solve your own problems."*

༥

Paul & Gean Young
Married: August 27, 1946
Marion, Ohio

Paul and Gean met at the "Hiway Rollerina." "Part of having a happy marriage is developing similar interests," says Paul. He and Gean both enjoy traveling, boating, bike rides, and just being together outdoors.

Hint #7

"Learn to bend and not break."

Gerald & Evelyn Smith
Married: May 2, 1946
Oklahoma City, Oklahoma

Gerald and Evelyn met soon after he returned from World War II. Evelyn was renting a duplex from his parents, and Gerald came to fix the oven. "He just wouldn't leave, so I asked him for supper," says Evelyn. "He still wouldn't leave — so I married him!"

Hint #8

❧

"Love always takes maintenence — kindness is a big part of that!"

❧

Merle & Evelyn Lashey
Married: December 20, 1946
Marion, Ohio

Merle and Evelyn well remember the moment they first saw each other. Merle was a basketball player, Evelyn a cheerleader for the rival school. Their eyes met, and needless to say, Merle played a great game that night!

Hint #9

"Do everything together, and make the best of what you've got."

Robert & Bette Barto
Married: July 18, 1946
Chicago, Illinois

Robert and Bette are seldom apart and remain very active socially. They're also proud that for over fifty years, they've spent every Christmas Eve with their sons!

Hint #10

"Don't expect to have everything right at the start."

M.L. "Dutch" & Lula Mae Noah
Married: March 27, 1946
Centerton, Arkansas

Dutch and Lula Mae believe a good marriage grows over time. "Dutch was a milk-hauler for forty-one years," says Lula Mae. "We didn't have much at first, but we had each other." "Marriage, children, grandchildren — what more could a man want from life?" asks Dutch.

Hint #11

〜

*"Everyone has problems —
just stay together and work
them out!"*

〜

John & Clarice Gillespie
Married: March 5, 1945
Phoenix, Arizona

Since John was in the army when they met, Clarice had to work. When he got out, she continued working to put him through school. "Our long marriage is just good economics," quips Clarice. "I had to stick around to get my money's worth!"

Hint #12

∽

"Always be best friends with your partner."

∽

Lowell & Lorraine Barber
Married: October 23, 1945
Two Buttes, Colorado

Lowell and Lorraine have a knack for keeping friendships in the family. "Two of my good friends married two of his brothers," Lorraine says proudly. Lowell raises exotic chickens while Lorraine likes to cook — but not his chickens! "That's not allowed," she laughs.

Hint #13

❧

"Really get to know each other <u>before</u> you marry."

❧

Howard & Barbara Rampton
Married: December 20, 1945
Sydney, Australia

Howard and Barbara did most of their courting long distance. "She was in Sydney and I was working in Victoria — 600 miles away!" Howard says. Since their marriage, they've enjoyed traveling to many different places including Spain, Tahiti, Scandinavia, Singapore, and England.

Hint #14

*"If you speak in haste,
then apologize with haste, too!"*

Bill & June Vogt
Married: March 30, 1944
Takoma Park, Maryland

Bill and June met in college. "He asked me for a date as I was coming out of class," June remembers. She adds that they have been friends from the very beginning of their relationship. Today they enjoy landscaping and reading together.

Heart Warmers!
(Tips from couples who know!)

"Take a quiet walk together in the woods."

"Have a picnic breakfast in the backyard."

"Watch an old movie together."

"Cuddle up in a hammock in the shade."

Hint #15

❧

"Always be honest, faithful, and true to each other."

❧

Ralph & Hilda Stanberry
Married: December 27, 1944
Rabun County, Georgia

Ralph and Hilda grew up in the same "holler" in North Carolina. "He used to think I was a nuisance when we were five, but not anymore," Hilda says with a grin.

Hint #16

⌒

"Remember, the Golden Rule also applies to your spouse!"

⌒

Gerald & Geneva Clark
Married: October 27, 1944
Spartanburg, South Carolina

Gerald and Geneva grew up a mountain apart. Twice a week for five years, Gerald walked the fourteen miles between mountains to "court" Geneva. "I was afraid if I wasn't persistent, someone else would get her," he says. They enjoy reading and taking walks together.

Hint #17
↬

"Never consider getting 'unmarried' as an option!"

↬

Art & Angie Grumbine
Married: February 5, 1944
Tujunga, California

Art and Angie have thirteen children. They say the secret for a long marriage is the same as for any other decision: "Ask yourself what God would have you do."

Hint #18

*"Share responsibility. She was boss
the first fifty years — I've got
the next fifty!"*

Lawrence & Glenyce Jensen
Married: September 23, 1944
Sac City, Iowa

Lawrence and Glenyce first met when he offered her a ride on a Harley he was taking care of for his brother, who was in the military. For their honeymoon, they drove forty-three miles to Fort Dodge — in spite of gas rationing and a strictly enforced thirty-five-mile-per-hour speed limit!

Hint #19

"Give each other plenty of space to grow."

David & Mildred Garner
Married: June 11, 1944
National City, California

David met Mildred when she was an aircraft riveter and he was a marine. "It takes a lot of grit and grace to keep a marriage together," laughs Mildred. The Garners raised seven children and are proud of their family — especially their twenty great-grand-children!

Hint #20

❧

"Agree that it's okay to disagree."

❧

Bill & Rachel Bergherm
Married: April 6, 1944
Takoma Park, Maryland

Bill and Rachel met in the kitchen of the hospital where they were working their way through college. Today they enjoy traveling to third-world countries to help build churches and schools.

Hint #21

‿

"When you get into an argument, take a good long walk to cool down."

‿

Melvin & Margaret Elliston
Married: June 12, 1944
Tacoma Park, Maryland

Melvin and Margaret met in a college art class. "The truth is, I came to college to get a degree, and she came to college to get me," Melvin laughs. Both love sharing the vegetables and flowers on their North Carolina farm. "He plants them and I pick them," Margaret adds.

Hint #22

〜

"Talk things out and never give up!"

〜

Delbert & Wanda Wilkins
Married: January 9, 1943
Lawton, Oklahoma

Delbert and Wanda have had a busy life with eight children and a successful business. "You can talk and pray your way through most problems," says Wanda. "And you don't have to *say* everything that you're *thinking*," Delbert adds with a laugh.

Hint #23

"Marriage is not fifty/fifty — you both have to be willing to give more."

❦

Ray & Gloria Ferry
Married: February 28, 1943
Las Vegas, Nevada

Ray and Gloria operated a successful business together, allowing them to spend far more time with each other than most couples. In addition to their other activities, they still take time to play golf together at least twice each week.

Hint #24

"If your spouse gets bossy, just stay sweet."

Willard & Estelle Church
Married: December 7, 1943
Houston, Texas

Willard and Estelle were born in the same town and met in the fourth grade. Willard served as a medic in the Philippines and Korea, later building homes and operating a broom-making business. Estelle spent twenty-five years working in a bakery.

Hint #25

∽

"Let life's experiences draw you closer to each other."

∽

Herman & Mary Sue Davis
Married: October 5, 1943
Greenville, South Carolina

Herman and Mary Sue sat next to each other in the high school band. "I played sax, she played flute — and we shared a music stand!" says Herman. Today they share many things, such as working together to compile the family genealogy.

Hint #26

"Watch how a prospective spouse's family treats one another."

Clifford & Carol Clark
Married: July 14, 1943
Stone, Saskatchewan, Canada

Clifford met Carol when he took eggs from his farm to sell to her mother. His visits continued and eventually he wound up with more than egg money! The couple is now retired from farming and cattle ranching, but still enjoys helping out on their son's wheat farm.

Hint #27

*"You can do everything together —
even shopping!"*

∽

Bill & Ruthe Ambler
Married: June 27, 1943
Utica, New York

Bill and Ruthe first caught each other's eye in a college wood-working class. "We started with very little, living in a tent while we worked at revival meetings," Ruthe remembers. They've now retired to a lovely mountain home and enjoy brousing local flea markets.

Hint #28

~

"Learn to be unselfish. Always put the other's interests first."

~

Claude & Elizabeth Steen
Married: March 25, 1943
Alahambra, California

Claude and Elizabeth met at an all-girls' summer camp where he was helping his mother. "I wrote in Elizabeth's autograph book, 'Hope I get to know you better someday.' And I certainly did!"

Hint #29

"Never go to sleep at night without saying, 'I love you' — and meaning it!"

Robert & Rachel Stewart
Married: June 14, 1943
Atlanta, Georgia

Robert and Rachel met at his brother's wedding. "It was love at first sight for me," Robert says with a grin, "but Rachel took a little convincing."

Hint #30

❧

*"You have to like each other —
not just be able to talk, but
really communicate!"*

❧

Sam & Mae Richiusa
Married: May 23, 1942
Yuma, Arizona

Sam and Mae are both children of Italian immigrants. They fell in love when they were very young and eloped as soon as they were old enough.

Hint #31

~

"Always be totally honest and open with each other."

~

Paul & Georgia Bateman
Married: March 14, 1942
Anadarko, Oklahoma

Paul and Georgia did a lot of talking before they were married and have never stopped. "Doesn't matter if it's big or small," says Georgia. "We talk over everything." When Paul returned from World War II (with four bronze stars), they bought a farm and began a small dairy.

Hint #32

"Keep your love, your health, and your faith in God strong."

Robert & Gladys Patterson
Married: June 14, 1942
Liberal, Kansas

Robert and Gladys met when he worked on a harvest crew. "I came in mostly asleep after running the combine all night," Robert laughs, "and Gladys gave me a cup of coffee — with a teaspoon of salt in it!" "I don't know what got into me," Gladys says, "but at least he noticed me!"

Hint #33

"Cooperation is the most important thing in a marriage."

Milton & Catherine Ewald
Married: November 25, 1942
Warwick, Rhode Island

Milton and Catherine are active seniors. Milton bikes and Catherine swims. "When you get upset, just don't talk at all." Milton joked, "Eventually, you'll get lonesome and forget what you were fighting about!"

Hint #34

❧

"Realize that neither of you is perfect."

❧

John & Ida Mae Freeman
Married: November 17, 1942
Kissimmee, Florida

John and Ida Mae met on a double date. "She was with the other fella," John says laughing. They enjoy traveling around the country in their motor home, especially to visit their ten grandchildren.

Hint #35

∽

"Find interests you can enjoy together."

∽

Wharton & Corda Jane Sanders
Married: July 4, 1942
Hyattsville, Maryland

Wharton and Corda Jane discovered each other at a bus stop when he rescued her from a group of drunken sailors. "I usually didn't give out my phone number, but I made an exception in his case," she says with a smile.

Hint #36

"Agree to walk away when a discussion becomes too heated."

Ralph & Marion Austin
Married: December 24, 1942
Kansas City, Kansas

Ralph and Marion were married during World War II. Ralph served in the air force and survived thirty-five combat missions. Today they enjoy watching and feeding the birds together. Ralph grows a vegetable garden, Marion a flower garden.

Hint #37

"Having the same interests isn't crucial."

Bob & Louise Garnett
Married: May 25, 1942
Grinnell, Iowa

Bob and Louise Garnett first met when her father picked up Bob hitchhiking! Louise is very much a "homebody," yet Bob has a number of outside interests, including a weekly television show where he interviews older Americans. "I wouldn't say Louise *supports* my 'hobbies,' but she does tolerate them," Bob said laughing.

Heart Warmers

(Tips from couples who know!)

*"Go window shopping,
then buy ice cream!"*

"Go on a date to the zoo."

*"Light candles and listen
to romantic music."*

Hint #38

〜

"Cultivate the ability to see each other's point of view."

〜

John & Elenore Buchanan
Married: November 29, 1942
Great Falls, Montana

Elenore was a true "war bride" — she only knew John for two months before they were married. John, a retired speech professor, is an avid bicyclist. Elenore stays active with volunteer work.

Hint #39

"Spend as much time together as possible."

Weslie & Marie Stabel, Sr.
Married: August 8, 1941
Gage, Oklahoma

Weslie and Marie were introduced by Weslie's sister — a regular at the beauty shop where Marie worked. "We've had ups and downs like anyone else," says Marie, "but we always worked and prayed them through together." Wes owned a grade-A dairy for years, and still maintains hay fields.

Hint #40

*"Use the common sense
God gave you!"*

Raymond & Bernice Bates
Married: May 17, 1941
Gentry, Arkansas

Raymond met Bernice when she was a young teacher boarding with his grandmother. "Folks these days are in too big a rush," Bernice says. "That's one reason they have so much trouble." In 1947, Raymond bought and rebuilt the creekside house in which they still live.

Hint #41

❧

"Feel lucky to be married!"

❧

Lou & Marsha Vabner
Married: October 12, 1941
Las Vegas, Nevada

Lou and Marsha are strong believers in commitment and conflict resolution. Lou says if an argument occurs that makes you want to get separated or divorced, then you're not handling the situation correctly.

Hint #42

❧

"Always try to please each other."

❧

Leroy & Dorothy Walker
Married: January 17, 1941
Old Fort, North Carolina

Leroy and Dorothy are one of three couples created when three brothers married three sisters. "It might make for a confusing genealogy someday!" Leroy says laughing. The couple enjoys camping, reading, and playing table games.

Hint #43

"Don't get mad over little things — they'll soon pass."

∽

Gerald & Helen Brown
Married: July 20, 1941
Fairview, Illinois

Gerald and Helen first "got cozy" when he drew her name at a Valentine's party. "Actually, it was more of a box supper — and I'm still fixing him supper every night!" Helen jokes. In addition to sharing meals, the two enjoy playing card games together.

Hint #44

~

"Forget TV and spend time with each other."

~

Joe & Pauleen Karner
Married: July 8, 1940
Mesilla Park, New Mexico

Joe and Pauleen started having "family worship" the night they were married. A few years later, Joe became a minister. Pauleen loves the piano (she taught for twelve years); Joe enjoys gardening and "inventing things" in his workshop.

Hint #45

"Spend quality time together every day — even if it's just a few minutes."

Ron & Sally Metsbeth
Married: May 7, 1940
Gallup, New Mexico

Ron and Sally first met at a church social. "And we've been pretty sociable ever since!" Sally laughs. Both are avid Scrabble players.

Hint #46

~

"Don't take things too seriously."

~

Curt & Jonnie Palat
Married: April 7, 1940
Greenville, South Carolina

Curt and Jonnie met at the grocery store. "I invited her to church," Curt says, "and we still go to church together today!" They often spend their mornings looking into each other's eyes over danish at McDonalds.

Hint #47

"Always keep your communication open and honest."

Ralph & Earline Moore
Married: August 29, 1940
Madison, Tennessee

Ralph and Earline got acquainted during a Saturday night college social. "He claims when I came into the room, he knew I was the girl he was to marry," she says. Both share a lifelong love of traveling and still manage to take at least four or five trips a year.

Hint #48

❧

"Never be the first one to get angry."

❧

Knud & Ruth Hansen
Married: April 9, 1940
Copenhagen, Denmark

Knud and Ruth dated during World War II. Because she was from Norway and living in Denmark, their love letters were censored by the government. According to Ruth, "They were going to deport me, so we had to get married!" She adds that they've been in love all their lives, and enjoy walking together and visiting friends.

Hint #49

❧

"When you marry, commit for a lifetime!"

❧

Herman & Bernice Walker
Married: June 9, 1940
Old Fort, North Carolina

Herman and Bernice met when she was fourteen and he was nineteen. "Some of the other boys would get fresh," she remembers, "but Herman was always a perfect gentleman." The couple enjoys gardening and listening to country music.

Hint #50

"Learn how to talk things over."

Kermit & LaRue Burrough
Married: June 15, 1939
Berryville, Arkansas

Kermit and LaRue have spent their lives operating a dairy and strawberry farm established by his parents. "Country life is ideal," says LaRue, "especially if you can find a man like my Kermit — kind, honest, clean living, and a hard worker."

Hint #51

⌁

"Learn to love and appreciate the good in each other."

⌁

Joseph & Lenora Holland
Married: November 2, 1939
Watts, Oklahoma

Joseph and Lenora are "complete opposites in disposition," yet have learned to work together toward common goals. Joseph was a carpenter when they married, served in World War II as a combat engineer, and later became a pastor. "You must always love and appreciate each other," says Lenora.

Hint #52

⌐

"Always respect one another."

⌐

B.J. & Anita Kohler
Married: August 27, 1939
Copenhagen, Denmark

B.J. and Anita were married in Europe just one week before the outbreak of World War II. Today, they travel frequently and enjoy visiting with friends.

Hint #53

"If you can't change something, learn to live with it."

Kermit & Phyllis Foss
Married: January 21, 1939
Minneapolis, Minnesota

Kermit and Phyllis believe that opposites attract for a reason. "He's always calming me down," says Phyllis, "or I would have burned out years ago!" Kermit is an ordained minister, and over the years, they've served in fourteen different states.

Hint #54

"Learn from others. Good family role models can help."

Albert & Ophelia Rodarte
Married: November 29, 1939
Watts, California

Both Albert and Ophelia's families provide good examples. Ophelia's sister was married to Albert's brother for fifty-three years. Her parents were also married for life, and her dad lived to age ninety-three.

Hint #55

"Marry a hard worker and good provider."

~

James & Rosa Belle Clemmons
Married: January 21, 1938
Etowah, North Carolina

James and Rosa Belle met through her father. "He worked in Daddy's cotton mill," she says. "Daddy hired him, and I married him!" Both have enjoyed many years of fishing and going on picnics.

Hint #56

*"Learn to be content
with what you have."*

Culver & Virginia Wilber
Married: June 16, 1938
Urbandale, Michigan

Culver and Virginia got together because Culver decided that she "was the one." "He picked me out first," Virginia adds, "and I fell for him later!" Their evening routine includes watching the news while they eat supper, then watching Jeopardy.

Heart Warmers

(Tips from couples who know!)

*"Attend a concert in the park —
or make your own!"*

*"Snuggle under a
blanket by a campfire."*

*"Take a leisurely drive
and enjoy the scenery."*

Hint #57

~

"Spend quality time with your spouse and children."

~

Kenneth & Dorothy Emerson
Married: June 19, 1938
Angwin, California

Kenneth and Dorothy sat next to each other alphabetically in school. Dorothy says that even though their interests differ, "It's fun to hear what the other's doing!" One hobby they *do* share is getting lost driving together on country roads.

Hint #58

*"Learn to roll with the punches.
Do everything you can
to express your love."*

Lennie & Victoria Shane
Married: January 29, 1938
Tujunga, California

Lennie is a real-life cowboy who has worked horses and livestock all his life. A man of few words, his silence is beautifully balanced by his wife Victoria's shining sense of humor.

Hint #59

*"Focus on the things
that matter, and let
the little things slide."*

Tex & Donnetta Taylor
Married: December 12, 1938
Dallas, Texas

Tex and Donnetta were born in the same town just a few days apart.
They still remember playing together as children in her backyard.

Hint #60

~

"Keep two cozy chairs side by side, and enjoy time each day just sitting together."

~

Edward & Thelma Cogswell
Married: March 4, 1937
Washington, D.C.

Thelma met Edward at his parents' dry goods store. She'd stopped to buy a fancy handkerchief to match her party dress, but the store had just closed. Edward let her in anyway.

Hint #61

❦

"To have a good marriage, work as a team."

❦

Ervin & Kathleen Langley
Married: June 21, 1937
Springdale, Arkansas

Ervin and Kathleen met in a blackberry patch between their Ozark mountain homes. Even though Ervin worked and Kathleen stayed at home with their five children, they still tackled everything as a team.

Hint #62

〜

"Pray <u>with</u> each other and <u>for</u> each other daily."

〜

Michael & Jean Duras
Married: July 15, 1937
Krakow, Poland

Michael and Jean met when she was visiting her mother's family in Poland. "Michael was a factory engineer," says Jean. "He heard there was an American in the area and wanted to learn English." After they were married, they lived in Poland for twelve years, then moved to Detroit.

Hint #63

"Busy hands make for a good marriage."

∽

Darrell & Ethel Elder
Married: October 18, 1937
Fayetteville, Arkansas

Darrell and Ethel have been farming all their lives. "I could do everything except shoe a horse!" exclaims Ethel. In addition to keeping up with a dairy and huge garden, Darrell started one of the area's first commercial chicken operations.

Hint #64

∽

"Don't try to change each other."

∽

Don & Gladyce Kroll
Married: July 2, 1937
Soldier, Iowa

Don and Gladyce first met at a high school basketball game. They still share a love of sports and often watch ball games together on television.

Hint #65

∽

"Never go to sleep angry.
Make it right, even if
you weren't at fault."

∽

Ralph & Dorothy Gustin
Married: November 6, 1937
Spokane, Washington

When Ralph and Dorothy met, she was a student and he was her principal. They were married after Dorothy graduated. Today their favorite pastime is working needlepoint. "Just give us some yarn and we're happy," Dorothy says laughing.

Hint #66

~

"Make sure your dispositions fit.
Don't just 'fall in love.'"

~

Walter & Theone Wheeler
Married: September 3, 1937
St. Helena, California

Walter and Theone might never have gotten together if not for her piano teacher. "I had planned a career as a pianist," Theone says, "but she pointed out that he might make me happier than my piano. And he has!"

Hint #67

❧

"Be each other's very best friend."

❧

Duncan & Gloria Eva
Married: July 4, 1937
Durban, South Africa

Duncan and Gloria have lived all over the world from Zimbabwe to England. They continue to share a lifelong love of reading aloud to each other.

Hint #68

∽

"Determine from the start that divorce is never an option."

∽

James & Mildred Garey
Married: December 26, 1936
Fulton, Kentucky

James and Mildred met at a high school play. "We both enjoyed dating in groups," says Mildred. The couple loves to camp and are currently driving the wheels off their fifth motor home!

Hint #69

∽

"Remember it's not important to always be right."

∽

Gray & Madge Burleson
Married: July 11, 1936
Burnsville, North Carolina

Gray and Madge met at a church revival meeting where he was directing the choir. "He is the kindest, gentlest person I've ever known," Madge says of her husband.

Hint #70

*"Enjoy the simple things —
like looking at sunsets."*

∽

Auburn & Louise Roland
Married: December 14, 1935
Leicester, North Carolina

Auburn and Louise did their courting on "walking dates." "We lived out in the country," says Louise, "and neither family had a car." Today they enjoy just driving around together, often stopping to eat out.

Hint #71

"Be able to compromise when there is a difference of opinion."

Irving & Betty Filler
Married: September 15, 1935
Baltimore, Maryland

Irving and Betty first met while he was playing piano at a mutual friend's home. "Betty's a very kind person," says Irving. "I've never heard her say a bad word about anybody."

Hint #72

❧

"Do things together <u>today</u> —
you may not have tomorrow!"

❧

Grant & Ruth Burch, Jr.
Married: August 3, 1935
Anderson, Indiana

Ruth stood by Grant through a series of heart attacks, a brain tumor, partial kidney failure, and the loss of five fingers in a farming accident. Despite these challenges, he was active in local and state politics for over fifty years, raised Hereford cattle on a 600-acre farm, and lovingly supported Ruth and their two children.

Hint #73

❧

"Make your marriage a lifetime commitment."

❧

Clyde & Lois Mae Franz
Married: June 2, 1935
Collegedale, Tennessee

Clyde and Lois Mae met at college when she broke up with a jealous boyfriend. "When I heard about it, I sent her a note asking her to meet me," Clyde says. "And she *did*!" The two enjoy camping, bird-watching, and "anything else that gets us out into nature."

Hint #74

❦

*"Keep your priorities straight —
responsibility ahead of pleasure."*

❦

Ed & Ruby Hallsted
Married: November 23, 1935
Fort Smith, Arkansas

Ed says when he was dating Ruby, he "tested" her by going to her house just after dinner one evening. When he asked if she wanted to go for a ride, Ruby said, "after I finish the dishes." "I guess I passed," Ruby says with a chuckle.

Hint #75

"Marry someone who's a good cook!"

Jeffrey & Lettieteen Blount, Sr.
Married: March 17, 1934
Opelousas, Louisana

Jeffrey worked in a huge oil refinery until his retirement. For over thirty years, Lettieteen carried lunch to him each day, making his noon meal a special occasion.

Heart Warmers
(Tips from couples who know!)

*"Curl up on the couch
and look at wedding pictures."*

*"Walk along the shore together
under a full moon."*

*"Share an ice cream
soda together."*

Hint #76

❧

*"Go with someone long enough
before you marry to know
who and what they are."*

❧

Wayne & Anne Barton
Married: April 7, 1934
Peoria, Illinois

Wayne and Anne first crossed paths working in the same business district. Anne says they dated a long time because of the Depression. "We finally decided it was *never* going to end," she jokes, "so we got married anyway!"

Hint #77

"Learn to put up with his little quirks — he's learned to put up with yours!"

~

Lloyd & Doris Mitchell
Married: September 1, 1934
Jay, Oklahoma

Doris first saw Lloyd as he drove his parents' covered wagon past her school on the way to a new homestead. "I told the other girls, 'that tall boy's mine!'" she remembers with a laugh. "And sure enough, he was!"

Hint #78

*"Put each other first. Do everything
with your spouse in mind."*

Clive & Dorothy Possinger
Married: November 29, 1934
Chester, Pennsylvania

Clive and Dorothy first became acquainted while he boarded at her
parents' house. They've shared a love of games all of their lives and
say they've never been too busy for a good game of checkers.

Hint #79

❧

"Work hard, but take time to play, too!"

❧

Herbert & Maxine Hatfield
Married: March 11, 1933
Bentonville, Arkansas

Herbert and Maxine started with a small gas station. Over the years, their business interests grew to include a car dealership, an insurance company, a car leasing business, and several large real estate holdings. "We kept busy," laughs Maxine, "but we always took time to play along the way."

Hint #80

*"First make a commitment
to the Lord, then to each other."*

Melvin & Maggie Smith
Married: January 8, 1933
Chandler, Oklahoma

When they were teenagers, Melvin and Maggie worked in neighboring cotton fields. "The rows stopped at the fence," Maggie remembers with a grin, "so with a little timing, we could meet at the end of each row!" Melvin was a railway mail clerk for over thirty years; Maggie is a historian and author of twenty-four books.

Hint #81

❧

*"Remember your vows.
They're supposed to be true!"*

❧

Ulyless & Zelma Ryburn
Married: October 21, 1933
Marktree, Arkansas

Zelma first saw Ulyless as he was rowing across a lake. "It was love at first sight for me," says Zelma, "but he dated others before he got around to asking me!" "I guess she just grew on me," says Ulyless with a wink. "Besides, I had more fun arguing with her than anyone else!"

Hint #82

⤳

"Don't be afraid to express your affection."

⤳

Gene & Francis Wood
Married: April 22, 1933
Byhalia, Ohio

Gene's first wife died of tuberculosis shortly after their fourth child was born. In 1930, he met Francis who was a widow. "Gene is a real romantic," laughs Francis. "If the kids couldn't find us in the house, they knew we'd be necking out by the barn!"

Hint #83

❧

"Believe that no matter what happens, things will work out right."

❧

Leo & Frances Jackson
Married: August 27, 1932
Gaffney, South Carolina

Leo and Frances were "married all our lives." Leo first saw Frances as she was walking down the street in front of his house. Frances says, "He grabbed his mother and pointed out the window at me and said, 'That girl's going to be my wife!'"

Hint #84

❧

"Relax, grow old and mellow together."

❧

Charles & Cassie Eldridge
Married: October 2, 1932
Tacoma, Maryland

Charles and Cassie met when he asked her date who she was. "He asked my boyfriend to introduce us, and that was that!" she laughs. They enjoy doing crafts together, especially making toy clowns to hand out to children.

Hint #85

"A good marriage is based upon complete trust in each other."

Boyd & Carol Shafer
Married: June 6, 1932
Iowa City, Iowa

Boyd and Carol first met "in the stacks" of the university library. Boyd later became Director of the American Historical Association in Washington, D.C. "We were always very close," says Carol. "I've had a very full and interesting life."

Hint #86

"Stay with it and you can always work things out!"

James "Oscar" & Beulah Scaggs
Married: September 28, 1932
Bentonville, Arkansas

Oscar and Beulah raised four children in post-depression Arkansas. Oscar worked at the hardware store for over forty years; Beulah worked picking beans and berries and later in the cannery. "We worked different jobs," says Beulah, "but we always worked together!"

Hint #87

*"Don't disagree immediately.
Discuss both sides."*

∽

Edward & Vivienne Tarr
Married: October 31, 1932
Capetown, South Africa

Edward and Vivienne met after she lost something while visiting his college. "He found my handkerchief with my name on it, and then he found me!" Vivienne says smiling. After retiring from teaching, the couple's favorite hobby became trying out new restaurants.

Hint #88

⌒

"Work together and always help each other."

⌒

Walter & Beatrice Crandall
Married: September 15, 1932
Long Island, New York

Walter and Beatrice were editor and assistant editor of their college newspaper. "We were always together," Beatrice says. "Because we liked all the same things, marriage was a natural conclusion."

Hint #89

"Treat each other the way you want to be treated."

Robert & Dollis Pierson
Married: September 2, 1931
Ocala, Florida

Robert and Dollis got into trouble at school a few times. "He was always moving my books over to his desk before I got to class," laughs Dollis. She adds that after they were married, he never went to sleep at night without telling her he loved her.

Hint #90

~

"Life isn't always sunshine, learn to survive the storms."

~

Guy & Mildred Harris
Married: June 6, 1931
Nowata, Oklahoma

Guy and Mildred have lived on the same farm in northeast Oklahoma for over half a century. Guy stays active with chores and repairs; Mildred still cooks huge holiday meals for the family. They're also the author's much-loved maternal grandparents.

Hint #91

"Don't ever nag or holler at each other."

Edward & Fern Willett
Married: November 10, 1930
Washington, D.C.

Edward and Fern ran children's summer camps together for many years. "It was like a long, paid vacation every year — well, most of the time," Fern says with a grin.

Hint #92

"Express your emotions, and talk things out."

Frank & Alice Mosby
Married: December 7, 1929
Nashville, Tennessee

Frank and Alice were introduced by Alice's sister while she was visiting her in Chicago. They courted by letter and telephone for over a year. "If you don't express your emotions, you're not really being human," claims Alice.

Hint #93

"Stay busy — then there's no time to argue!"

Carl & Oneita Johnson
Married: December 24, 1929
Siloam Springs, Arkansas

Carl and Oneita had to do their courting "by mail" since Oneita moved away after finishing school. She still has the "hope chest" she filled in the years before their marriage. "I had everything in there to start a home but the furniture!" laughs Oneita.

Hint #94

❧

"Settle in your heart that you're going to stick it out."

❧

Alex & Margaret Clark
Married: November 7, 1929
Vancouver, B.C., Canada

Alex and Margaret spent many of their dates ice skating. They still have both pairs of speed skates hanging in the basement. "Someday I'm going to have them bronzed," Alex grinned.

Hint #95

~

"Always consider your spouse's wishes."

~

Frank & Rachel Spiess
Married: November 29, 1928
Washington, D.C.

Frank and Rachel met and were married while students at college. After spending over thirty years as missionaries to India, they retired to the Smoky Mountains. They deeply appreciate the beautiful scenery and country living.

Hint #96

❧

"Share common goals."

❧

Bill & Minna Divers
Married: October 20, 1928
Cincinnati, Ohio

Bill and Minna met when they were being admitted to practice law before the U.S. Supreme Court. "We liked the same things, our backgrounds and educations were similar; we were very compatible." Minna was a congressional lawyer for over thirty years; Bill's many accomplishments are listed in the world edition of *Who's Who*.

Hint #97

"Make love and trust the cornerstones of your marriage."

Henry & Mary Lankford
Married: August 21, 1928
Gentry, Arkansas

Henry first saw Mary on a farm where he was spraying the orchard. A few weeks later, he asked if he could walk her home from a church meeting. "A marriage isn't much," says Mary, "unless it's based on true love and trust."

Hint #98

"Spend time looking for ways to help each other."

❧

Paul & Phyllis Current
Married: June 15, 1927
Sand Point, Idaho

Paul and Phyllis always tried to put God first in their lives. "We once bought an abandoned school house," says Phyllis, "and remodeled it into a church." Paul ran a small sawmill operation; Phyllis worked as an art teacher and landscape artist.

Hint #99

~

*"You've got to have love,
and you've got to know God."*

~

Floyd & Mary Dixon
Married: April 1, 1923
Fallsville, Arkansas

Floyd and Mary met while riding horses along the Buffalo River in Arkansas. Floyd ran a sawmill; the nearest town had less than a dozen homes. "I only worked for money once," smiles Mary. "That was so I could buy a new cookstove. After I bought it, Floyd said, 'Now you don't need to work anymore.'"

Hint #100

∽

"Develop similar interests."

∽

Charles & Mary Dresbach
Married: November 8, 1926
Amarillo, Texas

Charles and Mary traveled the globe together in his work as a geologist. "Charles was so patient," Mary says. "At first we had lots of disagreements, but he would always overlook them." Mary eventually fell in love with travel and even learned to like geology. "And then we had a lot more to talk about!" she says.

Bonus! Hint #101

*"Choose a neat and tidy partner —
it certainly makes life easier!"*

Ray & Vernal Augenstein
Married: October 14, 1926
Waldo, Ohio

Vernal kept the house spotless, while Ray maintained an immaculate yard. When Ray passed away, Vernal never remarried because, "I could never find a man as neat as him."

Bonus! Hint #102

～

"Don't fuss about every little thing. Work on being agreeable."

～

Cecil & Nola Critchfield
Married: May 12, 1926
Chandler, Oklahoma

Cecil and Nola first met as children, but weren't married until in their twenties. Cecil spent most of his life working for telephone and electric companies. "We never had much," says Nola, "but we always had each other!"

Bonus! Hint #103

❧

"A good marriage is give and take — but mostly give."

❧

Merywn & Freda Bridenstine
Married: June 25, 1925
Iowa City, Iowa

Merywn and Freda met in college and later developed teaching careers. "We never had a serious fight," says Merywn. "In almost every situation, we both *gave* instead of insisting on our own way."

Bonus! Hint #104

"Don't expect everything in your marriage to be perfect."

Russell & Virginia Potter, Sr.
Married: May 27, 1924
Elkhart, Indiana

Russell and Virginia owned and operated hardware stores for over half a century. Even though Russell, Sr. is now in his nineties, they still drive to church together every week!

Heart Warmers

(Tips from couples who know!)

"Lie on a blanket in the sun and just melt together."

"Cuddle up in front of a waterfall or fountain."

"Hold hands and watch the sun set."

Bonus! Hint #105

∽

"When faced with a mistake, forgive and go on."

∽

Ollie & Hattie Sisk
Married: December 1, 1924
Westville, Oklahoma

Ollie and Hattie went to school together in a one-room country schoolhouse. "We used to make music together," says Hattie. "Ollie had a guitar, and I played an old pump-organ." Hattie still remembers the moment Ollie sat her under a tree and said, "I want you to be my wife someday." She was thirteen at the time.

Bonus! Hint #106

❧

"Your roles must be clearly defined."

❧

Roy & Cody Derry
Married: November 26, 1924
First View, Colorado

Cody believes the ideal marriage is one in which "the husband is a loving boss and the wife his willing partner." She says her husband Roy fit that ideal perfectly. "He was so handsome, so smart, and so nice to me, that I never even *thought* of leaving!"

Bonus! Hint #107

~

"Take time to work through your problems."

~

Kimball & Genevieve Slaugh
Married: January 3, 1924
Logan, Utah

Because of his work with the federal government, Kimball and Genevieve faced the stress of moving often. "We've lived in such diverse places as Iran and Vietnam," says Genevieve. "It's been an interesting, and at times challenging, way of life."

Bonus! Hint #108

"You can always work things out if you really want to."

Earl & Ila McNair
Married: October 16, 1921
Siloam Springs, Arkansas

Earl and Ila met at a food booth during the city picnic. After they were married, Earl opened a plumbing business while Ila raised their two children and helped out in the shop. "If you can't get along *before* you're married," Ila advises, "you sure won't manage with the added pressures of a job and children!"

Bonus! Hint #109

"Work at becoming closer and closer."

Elmer & Emma Porter
Married: June 21, 1921
Oklahoma City, Oklahoma

Emma first met Elmer while he was working in a friend's barber shop. "He seemed so nice and was nice-looking, too!" she recalls. Elmer eventually owned his own barber shop, while Emma worked in a nearby grocery store. "We enjoyed just being together," says Emma.

Bonus! Hint #110

~

"Have fun just being together."

~

Arthur & Mabel Johnson
Married: October 22, 1920
Oklahoma City, Oklahoma

Arthur and Mabel met when he came to pick up his brother's engagement ring she was returning! "Six months later we were married," Mabel says laughing. During their seventy-three years of marriage, they took lots of little "day trips" and numerous vacations.

Bonus! Hint #111

~

"Never get too old to hold hands."

~

Arnold & Hazel Morelan
Married: February 17, 1920
Iola, Kansas

Arnold and Hazel were high school sweethearts. Known for their busy, loving hands, they "retired" by opening up a gift shop where Arnold cast concrete yard ornaments, and Hazel stitched handmade quilts and dolls.

Bonus! Hint #112

"Always treat each other well."

Theopolis & Martha Johnson
Married: December 24, 1915
Gravette, Arkansas

On their wedding day, Theopolis and Martha (Thee and Mattie) were accompanied by her sister. Not knowing the family, the pastor asked which girl was the bride. "Oh, it don't make no difference," joked Thee. "They're both kinda pretty, don't you think?" "I hit him," laughs Mattie, "and then we were married."

"Why, That's Nothing . . ."

Inevitably when a book like this is published, someone will write to us and say: "Why, that's nothing! Aunt Gertrude and Uncle Henry have been married ninety-five years, and they still go cross-country skiing together every winter!"

So, here's your chance to make your older friends and relatives famous (well, sort of)! If you know someone who's been married fifty years or more, just put together a short quote and biography like the ones in this book and send it to us! Be sure to ask their permission first, and include their phone number for verification purposes.

Who knows? They might end up in more *100 Hints: How to Stay Married for Life!* To mail your submissions or to write the author, address your correspondence to:

Bill Morelan
c/o The Concerned Group, Inc.
P. O. Box 1000
Siloam Springs, Arkansas 72761

Bill Morelan grew up very close to both sets of grandparents. Their "deep, loving commitment" to one another made a lasting impression on him, planting the seeds that later blossomed into this book.

Bill worked his way through college as a disc jockey, and later as a news director for a small-town radio station. He received his B.S. in Communications from Southwestern Adventist College in Texas, and his Master's in Education from Andrews University in Michigan.

After graduation, Bill began teaching high school (English, Speech, and Journalism) — a career that spanned thirteen years. Currently, he is Vice-President of Concerned Communications, a publisher of educational seminars and textbooks.

Bill and his wife, Sheryl, live in historic Siloam Springs, Arkansas. Between them they have five children — most of whom are now in college or graduate school. Their hobbies include "reading, getting lost on country roads, white-water rafting, and remodeling our turn-of-the-century Victorian money-pit!"

Every six weeks or so, Bill and Sheri spend an entire weekend getting closer to their favorite married couple — his grandparents!

Additional copies of this and other
titles in the *100 Hints* Series, are
available at your local bookstore.

100 Hints: How To Live To A Healthy 100

Trade Life Books, Inc.
Tulsa, Oklahoma